First World War
and Army of Occupation
War Diary
France, Belgium and Germany

16 DIVISION
48 Infantry Brigade
Northumberland Fusiliers
22nd Battalion (Tyneside Scottish)
1 August 1918 - 5 June 1919

WO95/1975/6

The Naval & Military Press Ltd
www.nmarchive.com
Published in association with The National Archives

Published by

The Naval & Military Press Ltd

Unit 10 Ridgewood Industrial Park,

Uckfield, East Sussex,

TN22 5QE England

Tel: +44 (0) 1825 749494

www.naval-military-press.com

www.nmarchive.com

This diary has been reprinted in facsimile from the original. Any imperfections are inevitably reproduced and the quality may fall short of modern type and cartographic standards.

© **Crown Copyright**
Images reproduced by permission of The National Archives, London, England, 2015.

Contents

Document type	Place/Title	Date From	Date To
Heading	1975/6 22 Battalion Northumberland Fusiliers Aug 18-Feb 19		
Heading	16th Division 48th Infy Bde 22nd Bn North'd Fus 1918 Aug To Feb 1919		
Miscellaneous	G.H.Q 3rd Echelon	30/09/1918	30/09/1918
War Diary	Boulogne Samar Desvres	01/08/1918	20/08/1918
War Diary	Desvres	21/08/1918	22/08/1918
War Diary	Noeux-Les-Mines	22/08/1918	01/09/1918
War Diary	Cambrin Sector	01/09/1918	30/09/1918
War Diary	Ref. Map 44.a 1/40.000	01/10/1918	31/10/1918
War Diary	Ref Map Tournai. Nos	01/11/1918	30/11/1918
War Diary	Templeuve Ref Map Tournai 5	01/12/1918	31/01/1919
War Diary	Templeuve	02/02/1919	24/02/1919
War Diary	France Templeux	01/06/1919	01/06/1919
War Diary	Dunkirk	05/06/1919	05/06/1919
Heading	WO95/Stray/QQQQ		

1975/6

22 Battalion Northumberland
Fusiliers

Aug 15 — Feb 19

16TH DIVISION
48TH INFY BDE

22ND BN NORTH'D FUS.

AUG - ~~DEC~~ 1918

1918 AUG to FEB 1919

From 34 DIV 102 BDE

16/c90 24

D.A.G.
   G.H.Q.
      3rd Echelon.

Ref. your No 140/452 d/18-9-18.

Herewith War Diary for month of August.
War Diary for June is being made up & will follow

Sept. 21st 1918

J. T. James Lt. Col.
Commdg. 22nd Northd. Fus.

Aug '18
Dec '18

22 NF Sheet 13 pt iv.
WSC 29

WAR DIARY or INTELLIGENCE SUMMARY

Army Form C. 2118.

Place	Date	Hour	Summary of Events and Information	Remarks and references to Appendices
BOULOGNE	1918 Aug 1	10 am	The Battalion left BOULOGNE by Rail en route for DESVRES	
SAMHR	"	12 noon	Arrived and detrained. Marched by road to DESVRES arriving there at 2 pm and taking over billets.	
DESVRES	2		Day spent in general cleaning up under Company arrangements	
		10.45/m	Enemy aircraft passed over the town — no bombs were dropped.	
	3		General Infantry Training and Specialist training etc.	
	4		Divine Service. The Division was filed to XXII Corps and formed Corps Reserve.	
		11.15/m	Enemy aircraft passed over the town — the bombs were dropped in the area. 6 Bombs were dropped in neighbouring town (SAMHR)	
	5		Commenced a period of Intensive Training under Battalion arrangements. General Infantry & Specialist Training. One Westernee Each Wednesday was reserved for Brigade Tactical Schemes and Route Marches.	
	6	11/pm	Enemy aircraft passed over the town — no bombs were dropped.	
	11	1/pm	Enemy aircraft again visited town without dropping bombs.	
	16		The Division was transferred to 1st Corps and was placed in reserve.	
	20	8.30 pm	The Commanding Officer and Company Commanders left DESVRES for reconnaissance of NEW AREA.	

WAR DIARY or INTELLIGENCE SUMMARY.

Army Form C. 2118.
Sheet 14. Vol 4

Place	Date 1918	Hour	Summary of Events and Information	Remarks and references to Appendices
DESVRES	Aug. 21		End of training. Special trench equipment was issued. Orders for move to Forward Area issued.	
		4 p.m.	The Battalion transport left DESVRES by march route to QUILEN where it bivouaced for the night.	
	22	M.N.	55 Boys stuffed by enemy aircraft - no casualties occurred	
		5 a.m.	Transport left QUILEN for CREQUY (LENIN Map.)	
		9 a.m.	The Battalion personnel entrained at DESVRES for Forward Area.	
NOEUX-LES-MINES		5 p.m.	The Battalion arrived at NEUX-LES-MINES.	
			48th Brigade here Divisional Reserve	
	23	5 p.m.	Transport left CREQUY for ANVIN arriving there at 10.15 p.m.	
		5 p.m.	Transport left ANVIN for PERNES arriving there at 10.25 p.m.	
			The C.O. and Coy Commanders made a reconnaissance of ASSEMBLY POINTS.	
		5 a.m.	Transport left PERNES for NEUX-LES-MINES and joined Batt. about 9 p.m.	
	24		The C.O. held a conference of Coy. Commanders, Second-in-Command & Specialist Officers. General Defence Scheme was discussed and arrangements made accordingly in case of enemy attack and Front Defences also carried out of all Ranks.	
	25	8.30 a.m.	Extensive reconnaissance was carried out of all Ranks	
	26	10.30 p.m. to 3.30 a.m.	Intermittent shelling of NOEUX-LES-MINES - 6 shells dropping in the camp including H.E. & GAS. No casualties occurred	

Army Form C. 2118.

WAR DIARY
or
INTELLIGENCE SUMMARY.
(Erase heading not required.)

Sheet 15. Vol 4.

Place	Date 1918	Hour	Summary of Events and Information	Remarks and references to Appendices
NOEUX-LES-MINES	Aug. 27	8.30am	Further reconnaissance of Reserve Defences by Scout in Command and Specialist Officers. A few shells dropped in NOEUX-LES-MINES	
		2.30pm	The C.O. held a conference of all Officers. Defence positions and duties discussed	
	28	7.30am	Scout, Lewis Gun, Scout & Signalling Officers made a reconnaissance of the FRONT LINE trenches, O.P.s & L.G. positions and signalling facilities	
		10am	2 Shells dropped in NOEUX-LES-MINES. Orders issued for movement to front line	
		9.30pm	The Battalion rehearsed the operation according to Defence Scheme, each individual being told & shown the exact position & duty. Explanation of scheme of Defence to all ranks.	
	29	9–12	2 Coys. fired on Range. Rifle & Lewis Gun practice in rapid fire and fire control	
		2.30pm	Baths. Sports. also S.O.S. Demonstration and aeroplane height flying demonstration	
	30	9–12.30	2 Coys fired on Range. Rifle & Lewis Gun practice in rapid firing & fire control. C.O. and Coy Commanders with specialist Officers reconnoitred Support section of Divisional line.	
	31		Battalion relieved 18th Gloucesters in left Sub-section & came into Bde Reserve for tactical duties. Daylight relief. W.B. Coys went on Front line, C & D. in Support	

Commanding 22nd Mcd. Co
J. Janson Lt. Col.

Army Form C. 2118.

WAR DIARY
or
INTELLIGENCE SUMMARY.
(Erase heading not required.)

Place	Date	Hour	Summary of Events and Information	Remarks and references to Appendices
NOEUX-LES-MINES.	Sept 1.		Ref. Map. Sheet 44A 1/10,000.	
CAMBRIN SECTOR.			The Battalion moved up to the FRONT LINE POST when it relieved the 18th Gloucester Regt on the LEFT SUBSECTOR, LEFT BRIGADE holding a line of posts. "A" Coy on the Left from Hastings Post A.5.d.9.6 to "B" Coy on the Right at the Mill A.21.a.65.80. "C" Coy in Support at MOUNTAIN KEEP A.21.a.5.0. "D" Coy in Reserve at PETWORTH A.20.c.75.35.	
	" 2.	night	Strong patrols were sent out along the front as the enemy were reported to be withdrawing. The enemy were located by each patrol and hand to hand fighting ensued, causing several casualties on the enemy.	
	" 3.	night	Active patrolling was kept up & 2nd Lt Orange captured a Boche prisoner, from whom we received some valuable information.	
	" 4.	2:30 pm	We sent out a daylight patrol on instructions from Brigade, under 2/Lt Gee J.T. Active patrolling continued. Situation quiet.	
	" 5.		Active patrolling continued & made preparations for attacking.	
	" 6.	5:30 am	We attacked with three Coys from Left to Right A, D & C Coys without Artillery preparation. The ground was very difficult, with men lying about. The weather was perfect with a slight mist. We gained all our objectives, "A" Coy finding the most resistance, they got beyond their objective and did very well. After the attack the enemy shelled our new posts very heavily.	
	" 7.		Enemy continued shelling our new line.	
	" 8.		The Battalion was relieved by the 18th Gloucester Regt and moved back to VILLAGE LINE as Support Battalion; while the 18th Gloucester Regt continued to push forward	

WAR DIARY or INTELLIGENCE SUMMARY

Army Form C. 2118.

SHEET 11. VOL. 4.

Place	Date	Hour	Summary of Events and Information	Remarks and references to Appendices
CAMBRIN SECTOR.	Sept 8.		We spent the next few days cleaning up & resting.	
	13		The Battalion moved up and relieved the 13th Gloucester Regt. in LEFT Subsector. D Coy in LEFT FRONT trench. 'C' Coy Right Front trench. B Coy in Support - AUBURN TRENCH. 'A' Coy. RESERVE LINE. Batn HQ. MARYLEBONE TRENCH. Situation was quiet and the men worked in their trench.	
	"14	8.30	Forward movement continued. General line gained. CANAL BANK. A.17.d.6.3. A.17.d.60.10. A.17.d.75.00. approx. S. to A.23.d.50.10.	2/Lt Martindale killed 14.9.18
	" "	5pm	Enemy counter attacked and we withdrew to jumping off positions.	Killed 2c M/Gs. Missing 15 ORs
	"15	morning	The Battn held line of posts from A.17.c.8.5 (Railway S. of LA BASSEE CANAL). Enemy Artillery normal. One enemy aeroplane endeavoured to cross our lines but was driven off.	
	" "	afternoon	Enemy put a barrage down on our Left Company which lasted about half an hour including many gas shells. Our artillery retaliated on enemy front positions and back area. Our own positions were shelled at intervals with Gas shells particularly LA BASSEE - CAMBRIN ROAD during the night.	
	"16	morning	Enemy very active behind his line. MGs and enemy posts located. Our artillery very active. Enemy shelled our positions intermittently throughout the day with H.E. & Gas shells. Enemy shelled LA BASSEE - CAMBRIN Road with Heavy Artillery & Gas shells mixed, last for half an hour from 6.0 pm.	2/Lt. Brown OD. Wd 16.9.18
		afternoon		

WAR DIARY or INTELLIGENCE SUMMARY

Army Form C. 2118.

SHEET 18 [?]

(Erase heading not required.)

Place	Date	Hour	Summary of Events and Information	Remarks and references to Appendices
	Sept 16		Enemy aeroplane attempted to pass our lines but was driven off with A.A. Guns on two occasions during the day. Three enemy balloons were up during the morning and at intervals during the day. Much patrolling was done by us.	
	" 17		The 6th K. Coy. (B) attacked and captured the enemy posts. 5 prisoners were captured 4 of which were wounded. The posts were consolidated & established at A.18.c.20.75 - A.18.c.25.65 - A.18.c.35.55.	2/Lt Mangra wound 17.9.18 2/Lt Little O.C. Killed 25 " Ward 12 " Missing
	" "	2.30 pm	Enemy counter attacked after a very intense bombardment in which many Gas Shells were used, and gained the posts. Hosts pushing the Company back to original loading posts.	
	" "	11 pm	"A" Coy relieved "B" Coy & without any Artillery preparation attacked and retook the posts (without a casualty) from MERC own artillery put up a protective barrage in half an hour. B. after the posts had to consolidate. 3 M.Gs. were captured together. The Baton was relieved by the 13th Coucester Regt and then relieved the 6th Somerset Light Infantry in Division Reserve in CAMBRAI VILLAGE	2/Lt Adams ? Joined 15.9.18 Lt Moore ? " Lt Lynn Scott " " 2/Lt Morris ? " Mitchell ? Joined 19.9.18
	" 18		The Baton moved and re organised & had baths in MINNEQUY.	
	" 19		The Baton spent the day in cleaning up. Instructions having been received.	
	" 20		General Infantry training carried out under Company arrangements.	
	" 21		General Infantry training relieved by 18th Gloucester Regt. Moved out to VERQUIN Area, via LA BOURSE - VERQUIGNEUL Road.	
	" 22	11.30am	A few H.E. shells were fired over the village. One civilian was wounded severely. No other casualties. The Baton was billeted in the village of VERQUIN. General and Specialist training was resumed and Special Class for Junior Officers	

Army Form C. 2118.

WAR DIARY
or
INTELLIGENCE SUMMARY.
(Erase heading not required.)

SHEET 10. VOL 4

Place	Date	Hour	Summary of Events and Information	Remarks and references to Appendices
1918 June	22		Formed. Received orders to move to DOUVRIN CAMP.	
	23		Usual training during the morning.	
		6 pm	The Battn moved by road to DROUIN CAMP in order 4 Coy, A.D, B & C Coys at 10 mins interval. Weather fine.	
		8 pm	All Coys arrived and settled in camp escorted by 6" Hour (Liverpool) Regt.	
	25		55th Division Wath'g Scm. Lewis Gun Class commenced. Officers C.O. parade at 2 pm. B Coy Lewis Guns with rifles and Lewis Guns on short range. Firers were received.	
	26		C.O. inspected Battalion by Companies at 45 minute intervals & Coml training carried out. Lewis gun inspection.	
		8.30 pm	Tactical operation was carried out in connection with aeroplane. The Battn attacked towards & captured a line of trenches from K.2.c.5.1 to K.2.c.6.3 & were consolidating when aeroplane flying over coperated on our position. The men had to show on aeroplane the positions marked on the map & was moved within a few new lines. Manoeuvre was taken by aeroplane from our front. The situation was successfully carried out.	
	27	10 am	The Battalion moved up to support & relieved the 19th Gloucester Regt. in supporting trench.	To O.R.B. formed 27.9.18.
			A Coy relieved C Coy 19th Gloucesters Regt.	
			B " " A " " "	
			C " " D " " "	
			D " " B " " "	
			Battn H.Q. BRADDEL POINT A.21.c.15.60. Sw lin of Repo trench renewed from 1 C.P. Mountain Ridge A.21.c.5.0. to USSEN KEEP C.3.a.9.3. 1 Ration in each	

WAR DIARY
or
INTELLIGENCE SUMMARY.
(Erase heading not required.)

Army Form C. 2118.

Place	Date	Hour	Summary of Events and Information	Remarks and references to Appendices
From sheltering point	Sept 29		Relief complete. Situation very quiet.	
		6-	B Coy on post on the railway. Station quiet. Work was carried out in Company area & carrying parties to FRONT LINE. Weather poor.	Moko Creek 28.9.18
		*PM	For Instruct to be carried on by FORWARD Battalions. A. B. Coys were held in readiness to reinforce. Weather good.	
		9.29		
		9.30	C and D Coys moved out of Forward Posts. A & B Coys retreated about 5 Ma enroute in capture many prisoners (seeing few and firing on enemy posts. Mark neither sure	

Capt.
OC 22nd Machine Gun

WAR DIARY
or
INTELLIGENCE SUMMARY.

Army Form C. 2118.

22 N. Two
Sheet 21. Vol 5.
Vol 31

Place	Date	Hour	Summary of Events and Information	Remarks and references to Appendices
Reg. Maps HILL 70 1:40,000	1.10.18.		The Battalion relieved the 5th Royal Irish Rifles in the out post line from A.23.d.5.8.to B.29.d.4.8. "A" Coy right front, "B" Coy left front, "C" Coy right support "D" Coy left support. Situation very quiet, slight showers at night.	
	2.10.18.	8 P.M.	Enemy withdrawing. The Battalion moved forward and coy got into touch with them, keeping touch with the flanks. The Battalion worked its way forward.	
		1200.	On the outskirts of HAISNES to the N. was S. of village.	
		1700.	The right coy had established posts in YENDIN – DOUVIN – LINE.	#OR wounded 3.10.19
		1900.	Left Coy established in above line from B.13.C.90.15. to B.26.a.6.0. with support Coy running N. to S. on LA BASSEE – HULLUCH Road B.19.a and C. where it relieves for the night.	Whitehill 121, VH19 looker "Edwards 30. Munskie 6 Bullion 16 table 9 Thornbury Wm.
	3.10.18.		Advance continued encountering a little opposition, we captured a few prisoners and 3 M.G's and at dawn our objective (B.14-1) was taken. During the afternoon of the night. Active patrols was continued throughout the remainder of the night.	June 13.10.19 wounded 3.10.19 6.OR
	4.10.18.		We continued to Push forward and met with sharp opposition from M.G's and T.M's captured the DYNAMITE FACTORY and BERCIDU and Pushing on towards the HAUTE-DEULE CANAL when within 300 yards of Canal we consolidated Active patrolling resumed during the night. During the days operations we captured 15 prisoners and 2 M.G's. Enemy shelled BILLY and BERCIDY very heavily at intervals.	Artkull 1115 dog names 7.10.18 C.BERRITH 18.3.10.18 13.OR 10R Wells 4.10.18
	5.10.18.	night.	Active patrolling during morning and left Coy Pushes forward to some at B.14.b.9.2. where we captured 3 M.G. and 1 team. Active patrolling carried out during day and soft. We were bad Touch with the more forward friends by the 18th SCOTTISH RIFLES. Battalion moved back to the Blue line. AUCHY AREA as BRIGADE RESERVE	HOR de drowned

Army Form C. 2118.

WAR DIARY
or
INTELLIGENCE SUMMARY.
(Erase heading not required.)

Sheet 22 Vol 5.

Place	Date	Hour	Summary of Events and Information	Remarks and references to Appendices
Ref. Map. H.H.A. 1/40,000.	6.10.18		The Battalion picket and Lewis Coys had baths during the afternoon at CAMBLAIN. Working parties.	2/Lt Bowes ref. joined 5.10.18.
	7.10.18 and 8.10.18		The Battalion were employed in Salvaging and cleaning up old trenches. A great deal of valuable material was salvaged including munitions of every description.	Capt Smith. E.J. Killed 5.10.18. I.O.R.KilledS.O.M. G.O.R.-28 "
	9.10.18		We were relieved from AUCHY locality by the 9th ROYAL HIGHLANDERS and moved back to VILLAGE LINE from P.26.d.3.3. to A.21.c.10.70. with Batt. H.Qrs at A.25.d.75.25. on the Battalion commenced to clean up and collage all valuable material	I.O.R. dojnd. 6.10.15
	10.10.18		Training and reorganisation commenced under Company arrangements including General and specialist training. March Discipline and stocking Drivers were done.	Capt Scott.W.T. Joined 7.10.18 Lt. Ellis. J.
	11.10.18		Battalion training Programme "A" and "B" Coys employed repairing roads in AUCHY locality with R.E. supervision. "C" and "D" Coys employed on roads in General and specialist training continued	Joined 5.10.18.
	12.10.18		AUCHY locality. Church Parades and Baths for "A" and "B" Coys. Training resumed. Baths for "C" and "D" Coys.	2/Lt Eade. J.R. joins 7.10.18.
	13.10.18			
	14.10.18			
	15.10.18		Training resumed and Working parties. "C" and "D" Coys employed by 156 Coy. R.E. and 157 Coy. R.E. Further enemy withdrawal. The Battalion moved forward to AUCHY locality in support to 47th Inf. B.H.QRS. ROBERTSON's TUNNEL (A.21.d.92.).	
	16.10.18	1700.	Moved forward to VENDIN-DOUVAIN-LINE following up 47th Inf. Bde in Support to 47th Inf. Bde. B.H.Q. CITE DE DOUAIN	
	17.10.18		Moved forward to BAUVIN still in support to 47th Inf. Bde, where we billeted for the night.	
	18.10.18		Moved forward to LES-EPINCHELLES (PROVEMINT) and commenced work in filling in craters and clearing up trench ways up by the Retreating Enemy.	

WAR DIARY or INTELLIGENCE SUMMARY

Army Form C. 2118.

Sheet 23. Vol. 5

Place	Date	Hour	Summary of Events and Information	Remarks and references to Appendices
Ref. Map. H.H.P. 1/40,000	19.10.18.		Remained in LES EPINCHELLES and continued to work repairing and clearing roads.	
	20.10.18.		Moved from LES EPINCHELLES to PONT-A-MARCQ via ATTICHES where we were billeted. Divine Service and Special Meaning in the morning and in the afternoon.	
	21.10.18		Employed in clearing of roads and repairing craters.	
	22.10.18 to		The 27th D.L.I. Bde Band gave Concerts and Programme of Events was carried out including Inter Coy. Advance Guard and Outpost Training in the morning and Sports in the afternoon each day. Parties of men were employed in filling in mine craters and repairing and clearing roads & houses etc.	Prisoners Captured during month 210. M.G's 5
	25.10.18.			
	26.10.18.		Moved to Area N.W. of TEMPLEUVE. Location of Companies as follows:- B.HQ. LES RUES. T.10.6. S.H. "A" Coy. HELIN. T.3.d. "B" Coy. ARDONBRETZ. T.15.a. "C" and "D" Coys LA QUEZE. T.6.b.	
	27.10.18.		Sports were carried on during the afternoon in red billets. Working Parties for roads were supplied by "C" and "D" Coys under R.E. Supervision. Remainder of Battalion carried out an Advance Guard and Outpost Scheme.	
	28.10.18.		Working Party for roads consisting of "A" and "B" Coy with 2 platoons of "C" Coy. Road repaired between GENECH and TEMPLEUVE (Sheet Tournai No 5) 1/100,000. Remainder of Battalion carried out Advance Guard Scheme. Parties under company arrangements including Advance Guard Scheme.	
	29.10.18.		Battalion Outpost Scheme carried out as follows:- Ref. TOURNAI No 5 Map. 1/100,000. The Battalion took up position along a line HELIN-ARDOMPRE-LE FAYEL facing West. Scouts were posted and reliefs carried out. Battalion scouts being in opposition.	
	31.10.18.		Advance Guard Scheme were carried out under supervision of the Brigadier.	

J. I. ??? Lt. Colonel
Commdg 22/R No?dd 2.

WAR DIARY
or
INTELLIGENCE SUMMARY.
(Erase heading not required.)

Army Form C. 2118.

Place	Date	Hour	Summary of Events and Information	Remarks and references to Appendices
Ref. Map TOURNAI. 1/05	Nov 1st		"A" Coy at work on roads in vicinity of GENECH. "D" Coy working TEMPLEUVE, "B" and "C" under Coy arrangements at Divnce Guards etc.	
	2nd		Under Coy arrangements for Gnral and Specialist training	
	3rd		Moved to BACHY, and took over billets vacated by 14th Leicesters Regt. March 8½ via TEMPLEUVE, RAILWAY CROSSING, GENECH, road junction by X of COBRIEUX. Coy arrangements in Gnral and specialist training. C.O. and Coy Commanders made a reconnaissance of forward area.	
	4th		Further reconnaissance of forward area, carried out by C.O. & radio. Under Coy arrangements. Weather very wet.	
	5th			
	6th		Move from BACHY forward as Battalion in Support disposition as follows:- B.H.Q and "D" Coy TAINTIGNIES, "B" and "C" Coys at LONGUE SPULTE. "A" Coy at ST.MAUR. Marched via RUMES, PETIT RUMES, ELOIRE, TAINTIGNIES, where Coys were met and guides of forward Coys were carried on after dark. Weather very wet. TAINTIGNIES was subjected to mixed shelling for 15 minutes at 1500 hrs.	2.O.R. wounded 6/11/18 1.O.R. wounded 8.11.18
	7th		Working parties of two companies were provided by "B" and "C" Corps on main line of resistance. This party was heavily shelled but had no casualties. Weather very wet. Batt. staff in support. Made preparations for another move forward.	
	8th		Moved forward to keep tag R.I.F. but found that enemy had evacuated the position East of the Canal.	
	9th	0650	Erected bridge and crossed the Canal, obtained our objective, by 0600 hrs the objective was line of Railway from V.22.d.3.7 to V.15.6.9.9. Remainder of day was spent in patrolling.	

Cont'd

WAR DIARY
or
INTELLIGENCE SUMMARY.

Army Form C. 2118.
Sheet 25. Vol. 6.

Place	Date	Hour	Summary of Events and Information	Remarks and references to Appendices
	Nov 10th		Examining Posts were posted at every exit from ANTOING, which we had occupied, and Scouts made systematic search of all likely places for any Boche who may have been left behind.	
	11th	1100	Coys at disposal of Company Commanders. Armistice commenced. Under Coy arrangements for General and Special Training.	
	12th		Batt. Parade and Ceremonial drill.	17.11.18 2/Lt Mork to England
	13th		Company and Battalion Drill.	
	14th		Moved eastwards from ANTOING to TAINTIGNIES, route through BRUYELLE - WEZ VELVAIN - CUIGNIES. The Battalion was billeted in L'ECOUELLE with HQrs on arrival.	21.11.18
	15th		in TAINTIGNIES for the night.	2/Lt QS Black to sick
	16th		Moved from TAINTIGNIES to GENECH via CROISETTE - BERCU - FOURNIES, halted for dinner at 12.15 and resumed march at 1330 weather being bitterly cold. Billeted in GENECH CHATEAU and adjoining billets for the night.	24.11.18 (2) /Lt Davison /Lt Easton /Lt Hodge Jan 25th
	17th		Moved from GENECH to TEMPLEUVE Area, where four Companies were billeted. B. 3/c. Q at LES RUES.	
	18th		General clean up throughout Battalion.	
	19th		Platoon and Company drill under Coy arrangements.	2/Lt Moore to 1st R.I.F.
	20th		Company Drill and N.C.O.'s under R.S.M.	
	21st 16th 27th 28th 29th 30th		Ceremonial drill, Education classes and Recreation was carried on throughout the Battalion. Route march, Education and recreation. General Platoon and company drill. Ceremonial Drill under Battalion Commander.	

O'Allen Major
Comdg 22nd Northumberland Fus.
2/12/18

WAR DIARY or INTELLIGENCE SUMMARY

Army Form C. 2118.

22NF Sheet 26 Vol 7

Place	Date	Hour	Summary of Events and Information	Remarks and references to Appendices
TEMPLEUVE REF. MAP TOURNAI 5	1918 Dec 1 to 4		General Infantry Training. Commanding Officers Inspections. Education for 3 hours per day, also Ceremonial Drill.	
	5		Brigade Route march from Templeuve to Sonh-a-Marcq – L Save – Lakpee Froiaars – Tafruite to Templeuve. Three hours education in afternoon.	
	6th to 21st		General Infantry training as far as could possibly be carried out during the wet weather. Educational Training including Reading, Writing and Arithmetic (Elementary Technical & Commercial), Shorthand, French, Bookkeeping, Shoemaking, Tailoring, Carpentry and Shoesmithing, were carried out daily. Commanding Officers inspection, etc.	
	22nd			
	23rd to 31st		General Training as far as possible was carried out but owing to wet weather and Christmas holidays it was curtailed. During the month Sports of every description were carried out including Boxing & Football. Inter-Section, Company and Battalion competitions being held.	

Thomas ? Lt Col
22nd Northd Fus.

3rd BATTALION,
TYNESIDE SCOTTISH
(35th) (S) BATTALION,
NORTHUMBERLAND FUS.

WAR DIARY or INTELLIGENCE SUMMARY

Army Form C. 2118.

22.NF Sheet 27 Vol 8.

Place	Date	Hour	Summary of Events and Information	Remarks and references to Appendices
TEMPLEUVE REF MAP TOURNAI	1919 Jan 2		Battalion Route March from TEMPLEUVE to LE QUEZE - FROMPREZ - ENNEVELIN	
			PONT A MARCQ to TEMPLEUVE	
	3rd		Coy & Infantry Training, Commanding Officers Inspection terminal Drill	
	4/5	16th	Brigade Route March from TEMPLEUVE to ENNEVELIN - PONT A MARCQ to TEMPLEUVE	
	17th		Educational Training including Reading, Writing, Arithmetic, French, Bookkeeping	
	6.35	9	Shorthand was carried on daily. All Ranks available were on fatigue at TEMPLEUVE Station and vicinity	
	24th		Visit of both Coys Commander to the Battalion	
	25th		Lecture by Kittels by the Remounting Officer	
	26th		General Training was carried out. Salvage Parties were formed	
	6.30		to work at TEMPLEUVE Station	
			During the month Sports of every description were carried out including Football Cross Country Runs & Tug of War. 'C' Company won the Brigade Inter-Company Football Competition. 'B' & 'A' The Battalion Cross Country Running Teams took Second and Third place in the Brigade Cross country run on 10.1.19. R. Makinof won the 1st Weight throwing on the Brigade Boxing assembly on the 14.1.19 which occurred on 28. Pte Lyne was killed weekly. The Battalion band party performed in the TYNE THEATRE	

22 NF Army Form C. 2118.
33a
Vol. 9.

WAR DIARY
or
INTELLIGENCE SUMMARY.
(Erase heading not required.)

Sheet 28.

Place	Date	Hour	Summary of Events and Information	Remarks and references to Appendices
TEMPLEUVE	1919 Feb. 2	15.30	The Battalion was given an informal visit by H.R.H. The Prince of Wales K.G.	
	3		The Battalion was reorganized and four companies merged into one as, owing to demobilization, the strength of the Battalion had decreased considerably. The Coy. was in command of Capt. A.T. Davis	
	5	11.00	The Battalion paraded for presentation of colours by the Corps Commander.	
	16 to 22		All available men were detailed for fatigue parties at Templeuve Station	
	24		Lieut. McLeod M.C. and Lieut. Vaughan with 176 other ranks of the Battalion proceeded to join 36th Bn. Northd. Fusiliers for service with the Army of Occupation. During the fore-part of the month Educational Training including Reading, Writing, Arithmetic, French & Bookkeeping was carried out daily	

E. Jameson Lt. Col.
Commdg. 22nd Bn. Northd. Fusiliers

Army Form C. 2118.

WAR DIARY
or
INTELLIGENCE SUMMARY.
(Erase heading not required.)

Place	Date	Hour	Summary of Events and Information	Remarks and references to Appendices
England	June 1 1919	13.00	[illegible handwritten entries]	
Dunkirk	5			

WO 95/STry/9999

www.ingramcontent.com/pod-product-compliance
Lightning Source LLC
Chambersburg PA
CBHW081508160426
43193CB00014B/2619